Grandma Never Complained

Written by Jewel Nolden

Illustrated by Laura Martinez

Southlake, Texas

© Copyright by Jewel Nolden

Grandma Never Complained

All rights reserved. No part of this publication may be reproduced, in any form, or by any means, electronic or mechanical, including photocopying, recording, or any other means without the prior written permission of the publisher, with the exception of brief quotations embodied in a critical review and other non-commercial uses permitted by copyright law. For permission requests write to the publisher at the address below. Address correspondence as "Attention: Permissions Coordinator".

ISBN ;979-8-218-16252-8

Gemlight Publishing LLC
2600 E. Southlake Blvd.
Southlake, Texas 76092
gemlightpublishing.com

Ordering Information:
Special discounts are available on quantity purchases by corporations, associations, and other groups. For details, contact the publisher at the address above.
For orders by U.S.A. trade bookstores and wholesalers please contact Big Distribution:
Tel: (833) 436-5483
or visit gemlightpublishing.com .

Printed in the United States of America

DEDICATION

My Mother: Mother, you were a woman like no other. You gave me life, nurtured me, held me, kissed me, taught me, dressed me, fought for me, and most importantly loved my siblings and I unconditionally.
There aren't enough words I can say to describe just how important you were to me, and what a powerful influence you had on me.
Your Baby Boy, Willie Earl

Memories of Grandma: Memories grow and memories fade, but memories of Grandma never go away. Her smiles rest in mine, her hands help me, her love fills my heart, and her spirit runs through my soul.
Mama, I'll always remember your voice, laughs and joyful spirit.
Lamont (Grandson)

About My Mama: As long as I can remember my mama has always had her hands in a giving position, caring for others, and having an unselfish heart. I thank God for my mama being an amazing person in my life. During the Christmas, my mama gave each of her grandchildren their personal gift.
Who Are You: You are the one who I looked forward to visiting on Sunday after church. You were the person who enjoyed fishing with friends, and sharing fish caught with us. My Grandma Lucille, I'm so blessed to have had you in my life.
Melvin (granddaughter).

Mama Lucille, you'll always hold a special place in my heart. I thank God for you, and the unconditional love you gave us. I'm sure I speak for all of us, we'll always cherish your memories.
Thank you for being my personal Saving Account. Love You!
Shirley (Granddaughter)

MY GRANDMOTHER'S
Hands Symbolized Strength And God's
Anointed Power.

MY GRANDMA
Mrs. Lucille Briggs Thomas

> Grandma never complained of her hands positioned,
> and praying God's Blessings upon her family.
> On the plantation, Grandma's hands cared for her
> children, grandchildren, and children of her neighbors,
> and she never once complained.

Grandma never complained using her hands to wash dishes, laundry, cooking and cleaning her home.

Grandma used her hands and washed clothes on the washboard, hang them neatly on the line, and ironed them with homemade starch, she never complained.

Grandma's hands pumped and carried water into the home for cooking, drinking, and bathing her children, and she never complained.

Grandma walked and crawled down damp cotton fields, and using her hands to pick cotton. She received $2.50 for one hundred pounds picked, and she never complained.

Grandma never complained when using her hands to bake tea cakes and make homemade ice cream for her children and other family members.

On Saturday nights, Grandma used her hands to turn the radio station to WDIA Memphis, and listened to her favorite radio station, and she never complained.

Grandma never complained when using her hands to shake pecan and persimmon trees, and picked up nuts and fruits for her family.

Grandma used her hands to disciplined her children and grandchildren with a belt (not all the time, but mostly spoke firmly), and she never complained.

Grandma used her hands to assist her sister with milking her cow and churning for butter, and she never once complained.

During the coldest months of the year, Grandma sat with women who lived on the plantation and stitched lovely designed quilts, without once complaining.
This was an enjoyable time for the women, "No Farm Work."

Grandma used her hands and chopped wood for cooking and warming her home, and never complained.

On Good Friday, Grandma used her hands and planted different vegetable seeds, she never complained. During the Summer months, she picked cucumber for $0.25 a bushel, canned jars of fruits and vegetables, and she never complained.

Grandma used her hands and gave her granddaughter half of her tuition to attend MVSU during the Summer of 1972, and she never complained.
The granddaughter was thankful and grateful, and always blessed her grandmother after receiving her degree.

ABOUT THE AUTHOR

Jewel Nolden is a Sharecropper's daughter who has picked/ chopped cotton and picked cucumbers on the farm. She was born in Gunnison, Mississippi, on a plantation in her Grandmother Lucille's Shotgun House.
She didn't live on the plantation, however, witnessed her grandmother and other families' lifestyles on the plantation. Jewel is the oldest of eight children who lived with her mother and Stepfather, Thurman. During her childhood and young adult life, she lived in the Delta part of Mississippi.

Later, moving to Chicago, where she lived over forty years before returning to her Home State of Mississippi. While living in Chicago, she was blessed to established a relationship with her biological father, Walter Pope who has eight other children.
Jewel is thankful to God for allowing her to experienced life in the South and Chicago. She can write many stories of both places.
Jewel is a Graduate of Rosedale High School. She received a Bachelor of Science Degree from Mississippi Valley State University of Itta Bena, Mississippi and Master Degree from Concordia University of River Forest, Illinois. In 2018, Jewel
received an Honorary Doctor of Divinity from Atlantic Coast Theology Seminary of Daytona Beach, Florida.
Jewel's greatest passions in Chicago were teaching Medically and Physically Challenged Students nearly thirty years at Chicago Public Schools; evangelizing and sharing the Word of God to individuals on the streets of Chicago.
Jewel is a Retired Special Education Teacher, Licensed Minister, Actress, Writer, Radio Personality, Author and an Event Planner. She has planned family reunions and her hometown picnics in Chicago.
Jewel was responsible for the Historical Marker presented to Mildrette Netter of Alcorn State University. In 1968, Mildrette participated in the Summer Olympics in Mexico City, Mexico. She won a gold medal in Track and Field. While living in Illinois, Jewel contacted Mississippi Department of Archives & History regarding a Historical Marker for Mildrette. Fifty years were approaching, and there weren't any markers or evidences in Mississippi of Mildrette participating in the Olympics. On September 18, 2017, an Unveiling Ceremony of the Historical Marker was held on the front lawn of the high school
Mildrette attended in Rosedale.

www.ingramcontent.com/pod-product-compliance
Lightning Source LLC
LaVergne TN
LVHW070433070526
838199LV00014B/497